W9-BOE-686

Other Books by Karen Pryor

Nursing Your Baby
Lads Before the Wind: Adventures in Porpoise Training
Don't Shoot the Dog!

How to Teach Your Dog to Play Frisbee

KAREN PRYOR

Cartoons by Roy McKie

SIMON AND SCHUSTER
NEW YORK

Copyright © 1985 by Karen Pryor
Photograph on p. 64 by Rich Hein: © News Group Chicago, Inc.,
1984. Reprinted with permission of the Chicago Sun-Times.
All rights reserved
including the right of reproduction
in whole or in part in any form
Published by Simon and Schuster
A Division of Simon & Schuster, Inc.
Simon & Schuster Building
Rockefeller Center
1230 Avenue of the Americas
New York, New York 10020
SIMON AND SCHUSTER and colophon are registered trademarks of
Simon & Schuster, Inc.
FRISBEE is a registered trademark of Wham-O, Inc., U.S. Trademark Reg. No.
679,186, issued May 26, 1959, for toy flying saucers for toss games. The term
Frisbee, as used in the title and text of this book, refers solely to the flying discs
manufactured and sold by Wham-O, Inc. under the trademark Frisbee®. The first
letter of the word Frisbee is capitalized throughout this book as the method chosen
to signify that the term is a registered trademark. No use of the word Frisbee in
this book should be assumed to imply that Frisbee is a game or sport, rather than a
toy flying disc.
Designed by Stanley S. Drate/Folio Graphics Co. Inc.
Manufactured in the United States of America

10 9 8 7 6 5 4 3 2 1

Library of Congress Cataloging in Publication Data

Pryor, Karen, DATE.
How to teach your dog to play frisbee.

Bibliography: p.
1. Flying discs (Game) 2. Dogs—Training.
I. Title.
GV1097.F7P78   1985   796.2   85–2339
ISBN: 0-671-55552-9

Acknowledgments

I'd like to thank Irv Lander, Alex Stein, and their staff and volunteers, for inviting me to the 1984 Ashley Whippet Invitational finals in Chicago, and for their many kindnesses. All the 1984 finalists contributed training tips and know-how to this book. I greatly enjoyed meeting these fine trainers, their families, and their very special dog teammates. I'd also like to thank Bob and Carolyn Cox and Daryl Breese of the K-9 Disc Masters for their photographs and extensive information, and Don "Rocket" Hoskins for his suggestions and insights.

I'm grateful to Anne Rathbun and Mesa, and to Marcia Koenig and Orca, who posed for training pictures. My thanks, too, to Ted Pryor, whose training of Max inspired the book in the first place; to my husband, Jon Lindbergh, for his photography and for his patience with me, Skookum, and a houseful of Frisbees; and to my editor at Simon and Schuster, Don Hutter, who, over drinks in the lobby of the Algonquin, bought the idea of a book about Frisbee dogs.

Contents

CHAPTER 1

Dogs, Frisbees, and Positive Reinforcement

This book had its genesis in 1981, the year I spent for the most part in a New York apartment writing another book, an explanation of how to use the laws of reinforcement (which form the basis of behavioral psychology) in creative ways, in everyday life, to train both animals and people (*Don't Shoot the Dog!*, Simon and Schuster, 1984). I had learned my training skills working with dolphins at Hawaii's Sea Life Park. Unlike most domestic animals, dolphins can't easily be punished; you can't use a leash, a bridle, or even your fist on an animal that just swims away. Consequently, all dolphin training is done with positive reinforcement, following scientific laws generated in the laboratory but applying them with some imagination. As anyone who has seen a dolphin show can testify, the system works; you can train a dolphin to do practically anything, and the dolphins love it. Now, as a writer, I was struggling with the task of passing on to others the intricate and powerful rules of reinforcement training, rules that up until then had been pretty well buried in the scientific literature.

Meanwhile, my son Ted Pryor, himself quite practiced in the rules of positive reinforcement, was going to graduate school at Columbia University and living in a small apartment with a large golden retriever named Max. To keep poor Max from going to pieces, Ted took the dog to Central Park most afternoons and exercised him by playing Frisbee. One night when Ted had come to my place for dinner, he remarked that I was wasting my time writing a book about training everything and anything; what the world really needed was a book on training dogs to play Frisbee. It seemed that almost every time Ted and Max played Frisbee in the park, some other dog owner would stop him and say, "How do you do that? I can't get my dog to play Frisbee." The dog owner usually went on to complain that his pet would get all excited and leap for the Frisbee if the owner waved it around, but if he threw it, the dog would just stand and watch it go.

Of course Ted and I knew what the problem was: Teaching a dog to play Frisbee is not amenable to standard dog obedience training. Ted was right: The Frisbee dog trainers needed a book of their own. In obedience training, you make a dog do what you want until it learns to do it correctly, either to please you and earn praise or, more often, to stay out of trouble and avoid punishment. In playing Frisbee, however, the dog must do what he does to please himself (or herself; for convenience, I'm going to assume throughout this book that you have a male dog), voluntarily and, at first, spontaneously. The only tool you have to shape the dog's behavior is positive reinforcement—praise and reward for desirable actions the dog offers.

Let me tell you a bit about positive reinforcement training. Whether we realize it or not, we use positive reinforcement all the time: "Atta boy," "Good girl," and so on. But *training* with positive reinforcement involves a lot more than just using praise instead of punishment. To make the praise work as a teaching aid, to actually use it to change and develop behavior, you need first of all to develop correct timing; reinforcing too early or too late doesn't work. Then you need to know something about shaping (the art of bringing new behavior into being, step by step) and something about stimulus control (getting things to happen on cue). With these tools you can train virtually any species of animal to perform almost any kind of behavior.

Though reinforcement training may appear to be obvious and just plain common sense on the surface, it is actually rather contradictory to the way most of us were brought up. Most of us were taught to try to *make* things happen, and if it doesn't work at first, to try harder. In reinforcement training you don't make things happen, you *let* them happen, and you mark the more desirable passing events with reinforcements. It's a training system that calls for a sort of Zen-like passive awareness as opposed to force or interference. This is a novel experience for most people.

For all its ease and lack of force, reinforcement training is an extraordinarily powerful system. As I've said, there is really no good way to use force on a dolphin. But it's easy to train a dolphin to somersault in the air or to do anything it is physically capable of if the animal earns a payoff each step of the way, and thus is motivated to figure out what you want. The animal becomes a willing partner and in fact does a lot of the work itself. It would be impossible to provoke such skilled athletic performance through physical coercion or fear of punishment.

With dogs, positive reinforcement allows you to train behavior that could *never* be trained by force or coercion— that is, by collar and leash, giving orders and requiring obedience. A Frisbee-playing dog has to be free and away from you to catch the Frisbee, so you can't force him to do it. He has to place himself in the right spot, gauge the flight of the disk correctly, and leap and land safely. These are skills he has to develop on his own; you can't tell him how, you can only praise him for his progress.

There is another intrinsic advantage in using positive reinforcement with dogs when teaching them to play Frisbee. Frisbee-playing is a good example of what psychologists call a behavior chain, a series of actions linked together, and behavior chains have to be trained *backwards*; that is, to arrive at the complete sequence you train the *last* action first. In the

Getting airborne: Snow, a white German shepherd owned by Ken McCort of Akron, Ohio.   CAROLYN COX

case of Frisbee, the dog must learn to bring the Frisbee back before it can understand that it should go and get it. Behavior chains can be trained only with positive reinforcement, as we shall see.

Is Frisbee especially good for your dog? Why Frisbee? First, because the nature of the Frisbee's flight is enormous fun for the dog. I've known many dogs who liked to chase balls and sticks and bring them back, but unless they are easily amused nitwits, most dogs get tired of sticks and balls after a few throws (exception: retrievers, for whom fetching is life's main job). The Frisbee is different. When a dog has learned to chase and catch Frisbees, he is apt to become such an enthusiast that he will play until exhausted. It's the unpredictability of the Frisbee that makes it so attractive. Once a ball or a stick has left the thrower's hand, its trajectory is ordained: You know and the dog knows exactly where it is going to go; the only variety that might crop up is a bounce or two. But the Frisbee soars and floats, changes direction, dips suddenly, or even climbs; it acts like real prey. The only thing it doesn't do is deliberately avoid the dog, as real prey would; so the dog can be wonderfully successful in the hunt. And dogs love that.

Second, Frisbee-playing is excellent exercise. Many dogs, and especially big dogs living in cities or in the suburbs, never get enough exercise to be really fit. But if you and your dog can play Frisbee, it is possible to give the dog all the exercise he can handle while you stand comfortably in one spot thinking about the stock market, if you wish. Remember that exercise is just as important for animals as it is for people. Dogs were meant to run: if your dog gets the running he needs, he will be healthier, live longer, look better, sleep better, shed less, and be a more enjoyable companion than he would be if he were out of shape. Frisbee is an ideal way to make that happen.

Finally, I think Frisbee is good for dogs because it occupies their minds. That no doubt seems a wildly unscientific statement—to assume that dogs have minds. Nevertheless, from a practical standpoint, most professional animal trainers are convinced that the demands and excitement of learning and doing a task (a challenging session of work or training almost every day, even if for just a few minutes) give the animal something to think about the rest of the time and that this mental stimulation is highly beneficial to the animal's well-being.

The stimulation of a training session of some sort is especially valuable for animals who must be alone for much of the day while their owners are away at work or school. If your dog spends long hours shut up in your house or apartment, or on a chain or in a pen, then a hard, fast, skill-sharpening session of Frisbee now and then may help relieve the animal's boredom at other times. You may even find other problems diminishing or actually clearing up, such as prolonged barking, destructive chewing, and digestive disorders or skin rashes. For the lonely pet, Frisbee is good therapy.

And, in using this book to teach your dog to play Frisbee, you will be benefiting him in many ways. You will also learn something about reinforcement training, which you may find to be personally beneficial. It can lead to a whole new level of communication with your dog, a mutual understanding that can become an almost magical experience. Above all, as competition Frisbee-dog trainers like to point out, positive reinforcement training "kind of rubs off on everything else." The dog learns, yes; in no time you can use Frisbee play to turn a fat, lazy nuisance of a house pet into a fit, vigorous, alert, responsive and crowd-pleasing Frisbee dog. But even more rewarding is what you can learn and experience yourself; you may find many applications for positive reinforcement techniques throughout the rest of your life. Training a dog to play Frisbee is wonderful for the dog, but it can also be a creative leap forward for his master.

CHAPTER 2

Training

What is a positive reinforcement? It is anything a training subject wants enough to be willing to work for. Praise, petting, and food tidbits are common reinforcements for dogs. To develop behavior with positive reinforcement, you have to be sure you are using something your dog wants. It will do no good, for example, to lavish praise on an animal that doesn't care about your opinion (dachshunds come to mind) or is too busy with its own affairs to notice your approval. (In both such cases, food reward is especially useful, at least at the start of training.)

Very often, as training progresses, the behavior itself becomes its own reward. In teaching kids to ride bikes we usually use a lot of praise at first—"Atta girl, you got it. Keep going, that's the way"—but once the behavior has been learned it becomes self-reinforcing: Riding the bike is fun, and the child no longer needs praise to keep going. Frisbee-playing is self-reinforcing for dogs, although most dogs continue to need praise and approval to maintain good retrieves and to reinforce difficult catches.

The crucial rule for training with reinforcement is that the reinforcement must occur during the behavior or immediately at the conclusion of the behavior. This is especially important

First step: Donna Breese encourages Yote to jump for the Frisbee. Working on your knees often gives the dog more confidence. DOUG MILHAM

in the beginning stages of learning something new. The first time your dog reaches timidly for the Frisbee in your hand, your praise, "Good dog!" must come as he is in the act of reaching. A second later is too late. Late reinforcements have a weak effect on learning; only after many, many repetitions will the animal show improvement. Perfectly timed reinforcements work much faster. If you mark your dog's first timid reach with a well-timed word of praise, he may immediately reach again; after three or four tries, a matter of a minute or less, he may be jumping and taking the Frisbee with a very clear idea of what you want.

Reinforcements that come too early are also wasted effort; if your dog is not catching the Frisbee well yet and you encourage him during the chase with cries of "Good boy!" you may reinforce the chase, but you'll be doing nothing to improve the catch. In fact, you may see the catch deteriorate further as he decides that the chase is the action most important to you.

Conditioned Reinforcers

Perfectly timed reinforcements are vital, but what if we can't get the reinforcement to the animal with perfect timing, if the animal is out of reach of a pat, say, or has the Frisbee in its mouth and therefore can't eat a tidbit? In this case—which is most of the time, in practice—we use a conditioned reinforcer, a sound, word, or phrase we have especially set aside to be used as a training tool in lieu of the "real" reinforcement (such as petting, praise, or food).

A conditioned reinforcer communicates to your dog the exact moment that you like what he is doing, even if he is a hundred yards away from you. For the dog, this is valuable information because it helps him identify sure-fire ways to earn reinforcement. It is fascinating to see how a conditioned reinforcer—which is, after all, only a signal that real reinforcement is coming later—rapidly becomes a much more powerful reinforcement than a real reinforcer might be. A dog learns to work hard to earn that conditioned reinforcer.

Modern animal trainers often use a noisemaker, such as a police whistle or a toy clicker, as a conditioned reinforcer. With a household pet it seems easier to use spoken words. To establish a conditioned reinforcer, first select a word or phrase. In this book I use "Good dog!" but any words will do. You can say "Yippee!" or "Tuesday!" or anything else; as long as you are consistent, the dog will learn. Now you must consciously pair this word or phrase with real reinforcements, saying it once only, loud and clear, at the exact moment that you (a) set the dog's dinner down, (b) kneel down to make a big fuss over him, (c) let him in or out, and (d) give him any snack or treat. Notice that these instances are outside the training situation: You are merely establishing that "Good dog!" (or whatever) signifies good things.

Meanwhile, you must clean that phrase out of your casual language and *never use it again unless you mean it as a reinforcer.* Don't say "Good dog!" when you are chatting to the dog or romping and playing with him. Instead speak his name or say other words such as "Nice puppy"—something, anything, else. Keep your "magic words" specifically to inform him he has done something special.

Now you have a tool, the single most powerful training tool you can develop: a conditioned reinforcer that you can use to mark any new action exactly when it occurs. "Good dog!" when he carries the Frisbee toward you, even a few inches at first; "Good dog!" when he makes that first great catch.

As each step is accomplished and becomes routine, you can stop using your conditioned words for that step, and save them for new work and more advanced steps; the reinforcement is for learning the behavior, not for doing it when doing it has become easy. When you have given several reinforcements in the symbolic form of your conditioned words, be sure to back them up by real reinforcements, interrupting or ending your training session with "Good dog!" followed by a big petting orgy, a favorite treat, or both. (Incidentally, many dog trainers disapprove of food rewards, believing that too often you have to give it continually to make a dog keep working. By establishing a conditioned reinforcer, and saying it whenever you do feed the dog normally, you are using the highly coveted food reinforcements to strengthen the power of your praise words, and you may never actually have to give tidbits during the work.)

The Frisbee Chain

Playing Frisbee with a dog involves three separate behavioral skills: chasing the Frisbee, catching the Frisbee in the air, and retrieving the Frisbee so it can be tossed again. Only the last behavior can actually be reinforced by you, either with petting or another toss, but once learned, the chain is maintained because each behavior in the chain is reinforced by the behavior that follows.

It works like this: If the dog chases the Frisbee effectively, that behavior pays off by putting him in a good position to catch the Frisbee. If he catches the Frisbee, then that pays off by enabling him to bring it back to his owner. And if he does that, the behavior pays off by earning him praise and another throw of the Frisbee.

If a behavior chain is to be successful—that is, if it is to be maintained and not degenerate into "I don't wanna play any more" behavior—the chain, as has been pointed out, has to be trained backwards. Before you can expect the dog to catch the Frisbee *for you* (even though he might catch it occasionally for his own amusement), he has to know how to bring the Frisbee back, and that he will earn a payoff, or reinforcement, for doing so. The dog also needs to know how to catch the Frisbee in midair before he learns to chase properly; that is, he must know how to snatch it on the fly before he will be motivated to get himself out there where a catch is possible, instead of just trotting in the general direction of the throw and picking the Frisbee up from the ground.

And so, we train the Frisbee behaviors individually and

then put them together in reverse order. And since the individual behaviors are complex and do not necessarily arise spontaneously, we train each one by the method psychologists call successive approximation, or shaping.

Shaping

A shaped behavior is one that does not spring up full-blown but has to be trained in a series of little steps. You start by reinforcing the tiniest movement or vaguest tendency in the right direction. The animal is soon offering that small movement deliberately. You reinforce stronger efforts and ignore less vigorous ones: in due course the animal is making better efforts as a matter of course. Then you upgrade your criteria again and select only the better tries—until you have achieved the behavior you had in mind. This is how we train dolphins to jump twenty-two feet in the air or, for that matter, kids to ride bicycles. All three behaviors in the Frisbee chain—the chase, the catch, and the retrieve—are shaped behaviors. And since behavior chains must be trained backwards, we will begin with . . .

The Retrieve

Some dogs, especially Labradors and other retrieving breeds, will bring back anything you throw for them on the first try. All such a dog needs to maintain the retrieve is to discover that retrieving will be reinforced, sometimes by another throw and sometimes by petting and approval. If you have such a dog, give him his praise words each time he brings the Frisbee back, and follow up immediately either with another toss or with patting and approval—the two real reinforcers for the game. Be prompt in making your next toss. If the dog has to wait too long—say, while you talk to a friend—his fetch will go unreinforced, and his interest in the game may dwindle. If you are going to end the game and not throw again, make a fuss over the dog to reward him for his participation.

Suppose, however, you have a dog who does not retrieve spontaneously? There are a number of ways to shape the behavior. Some trainers advocate harsh training methods such as pinching the dog's ear until it opens its mouth in pain and then forcing the object into its jaws. But such methods are neither necessary nor appropriate when the goal is to have fun. Instead, you might begin with this simple method, right in your living room.

Use any toys or objects the dog likes to chew on or carry around (not bones; those are his property, and he is right not to want to give them up). You can use a Frisbee from the beginning, but if the dog shows avoidance of this hard, unfamiliar object at first, something soft such as an old pair of rolled-up socks set aside for this purpose will be fine too. What the dog learns—"My owner thinks I'm great if I bring him this thing"—will easily transfer to the Frisbee later.

Begin by tapping the dog gently around the mouth with the object. Wave it near his face, tempt him with it, and speak to him in an eager, encouraging tone of voice, saying, "Take it." (Remember, don't use the words "Good dog" just to encourage him if you are going to use those words as a conditioned reinforcer.)

You will have to see how your dog responds to this invitation to play. If the dog is a little bewildered or reluctant, it may be a moment before he responds; perhaps he has been scolded in the past for mouthing or grabbing at objects, and now you want him to do the very thing he has learned not to. In this case, watch for the least inclination to open the mouth or to try for the object, and immediately say, "Good dog!" and hug or pet him.

If you have a very eager dog who grabs for the Frisbee from the beginning, then play a different game: Pull the Frisbee away the first three or four times, then let him grab it and take it away from you, reinforcing and praising him very enthusiastically for doing so—"Good dog! He's got the Frisbee!" This

Eye contact with the dog and the trainer's clear, consistent signals enable the dog to anticipate the Frisbee's movements and ensure more successful catches. Tony Frediani cues his top competition dog, Duke, a Queensland blue heeler. KAREN PRYOR

will make the dog feel very successful. He may even swagger about, holding up his prize and keeping it out of your reach.

But we're trying to train the dog to bring something back, aren't we? Why are we encouraging him to steal it? The fact is that retrieving, *in itself,* is a behavior chain: The dog must take the object, carry it, and give it up. You are training those three items as separate bits of behavior, starting with developing the dog's interest in taking the Frisbee (or some other object) in the first place, and that is all we are working on now. (Ideally, you would start from the back of the chain and train the dog to drop the object on command first; but since he can't very well drop it until he's learned to pick it up, that must come later.)

To help the dog feel at home with the Frisbee, you may want to leave it lying around the house and let him use it as a chewing toy; dogs seem to prefer objects that smell of their own saliva. Some owners, however, prefer to establish from the beginning that the Frisbee is only for chasing, and chewing should be restricted to other objects. Others advocate giving the dog both his food and his water from the Frisbee. The theory is that the more pleasant associations he has with the Frisbee, the more he will crave to catch it.

Once the dog is mouthing the Frisbee when you tempt him with it and is trying confidently to take hold of it, the training path splits. On the one hand, you can now hang onto the Frisbee and permit the dog to play tug-of-war with it. On the other hand, you can also roll the Frisbee a few feet away and reinforce the dog with praise and applause if he goes and gets it. (Try to roll it in an arc so that it falls over with the rim upwards; this will make it easier for the dog to pick it up.)

Both of these behaviors are steps on the way to the Frisbee game. Going after the rolled Frisbee is a start toward retrieving. Tug-of-war develops muscle and jaw strength, and intensifies the dog's competitive desire to get an object and hang onto it. If the dog was not interested in the Frisbee before, learning to play tug-of-war with it will develop interest. (Be sure you let him get hold of the Frisbee with his back teeth, not just his front ones; it is very easy to injure the front teeth playing tug-of-war. Also, you must be judicious about how hard you pull, especially with a small dog.)

Keep-away

Sometimes, when a dog goes and gets the Frisbee or gets away with the Frisbee during tug-of-war, he is likely to start running around playing keep-away, trying to induce you to chase him and grab for his prize. We'll discuss later how to eradicate keep-away if it becomes a strong habit, as it can with some breeds, but usually the game will die down by itself, unless you accidentally reinforce it. To avoid that, never try to snatch the object; never get lured into playing this game unless you choose to. When the dog takes off, you stop playing. Go back to watching TV or whatever you were doing. Most especially, never give in to the perfectly natural human tendency to *force* the dog to give up the toy. Sure, you can probably frighten or cow him into stopping the keep-away game, but you will have spoiled the game.

Once the dog is going after the Frisbee, you can start training him to pick it up and then to bring it back. Keep the distances short at first. Go with the dog, if you have to, and encourage him to pick up the Frisbee. When the dog does go after a rolled Frisbee and picks it up, say your praise word and call him to you with much enthusiasm (getting down on your knees will lure the dog to you very strongly), take the Frisbee from him, and make a big fuss over him. If he seems excited, you can reinforce him further by rolling or tossing the Frisbee again right away and responding with much enthusiasm if he goes after it.

Keep the sessions short (five or ten minutes) and end them before either of you gets bored. If you get one retrieve the first time, that's fine; hope for three or four in the next session. If you find yourself getting mad at the dog for not responding, end the session at once. We all have off-days, dogs included, and it's better to stop a session than to induce bad feelings in either of you. Feel free to laugh and enjoy your dog's antics, even if he is being mischievous. Dogs hate to be laughed *at*, but they enjoy being laughed with; in fact, they love the sound of their owner's happy laughter. Don't get grim about training; let your dog know you are enjoying him.

Some novice dogs tend to pick up the Frisbee but drop it on the way back. In this case, keep the distance short and try to get in your "Good dog!" while the dog is heading back to you but before he drops the Frisbee. If you can reinforce him successfully for coming two steps in your direction, then four, then six, and so on, while still carrying the Frisbee, you will get past the dropping problem soon enough. Also, try running backwards while clapping your hands and calling as he comes toward you with the Frisbee.

Once the dog is returning the Frisbee (or the ball or the socks or whatever you are using) with some degree of reliability—say, three out of four times—you can then proceed with

the shaping by making the task more demanding. Here are some criteria you could add to increase your dog's retrieving skills:

Move the game outdoors (you may have to anyway, if you have a big dog).

Have him retrieve other objects

. . . or hidden objects

Have him retrieve over longer distances

. . . or when there are other people or other dogs around

. . . or *to* other people.

You may not want to go this far with retrieving, nor do you need to, to get the Frisbee game going; as long as the dog understands that he should bring the Frisbee back to you and that he will be reinforced for doing so, you can proceed to shaping the catch and the chase. But it is worth remembering that the more criteria you can add to a given behavior, the more reliable the behavior becomes under ordinary circumstances. If you have a dog who tends to fool around even with simple behavior, the remedy is *not* to keep drilling the easy stuff but to teach the dog more and more, so that carrying out the old, simple tasks correctly becomes a matter of course.

Shaping Programs

The plan described above for developing the retrieve is an example of a shaping program or a step-by-step training method. This is not the only shaping program for retrieving; there are probably as many shaping programs as there are trainers to think them up. If you are not making progress, you should feel free to try another shaping program or think one up for yourself. The only requirement for a shaping program is that the steps be easy enough for the dog to have a good chance of success at each new level. As a rule of thumb, the dog should already be achieving the new level at least half the time before you start insisting that he do at least that much every time to be deserving of reinforcement.

Here's an example of another shaping program, this one designed to deal with the dog who brings the Frisbee or other object back to you but won't give it up.

Step 1. Tempt the dog with the Frisbee or toss it. When the dog takes the Frisbee, grab him around the chest with one arm, take hold of the Frisbee with the other, exert a steady, gentle pull, and say, "Give." Reinforce any slackening of jaw; release dog and Frisbee.

Step 2. Repeat, reinforcing any increasing slackening of the jaw until the dog releases the Frisbee completely each time, even if it takes him a while. When Step 2 is done, go to . . .

Step 3. Shape for immediate release on the word "Give."

Step 4. Hold the dog but don't hold the Frisbee. The dog should drop the Frisbee into your hand on the word "Give."

Step 5. The dog comes and drops the Frisbee into your hand on command without any restraint.

A shaping program such as this should not be considered a hard-and-fast prescription; it offers guidelines, not rules. Say that during Step 2 of the above program the dog starts dropping the Frisbee at your feet. You might want to abandon the program and accept the drop instead. The point is that you can always devise new programs. If you decide, for example, that you want your dog to pick up two Frisbees at once or to jump over your leg while taking the Frisbee from your hand, work out a shaping program on paper and from that determine how to proceed.

A shaping program is also valuable in solving problems. For example, suppose you are working with a very independent-minded dog, using the shaping program above, and the dog growls at you for restraining him. You might want to work out a subprogram for training the dog so that he will allow himself to be held and handled, and add that to your training sessions as desirable behavior not just in learning Frisbee but in being a mannerly pet.

Also, a shaping program can always be extended. For example, having gone to the trouble to teach your dog "Give!" you might add . . .

Step 6. Hold your hand in the air and shape the dog to obey "Give!" by jumping up and putting the Frisbee into your hand, until he is jumping high over your head. Or . . .

Step 7. Shape the dog to retrieve various objects and drop them in a basket instead of your hand on the word "Give!" (and then use him to make an antilittering commercial for TV).

You get the idea. With creative shaping programs you can train for anything.

Shaping the Chase

Once you have proceeded with the retrieve to the point where you have a reasonable chance of getting your Frisbee back, you can start shaping the chase. The shaping program is very straightforward:

Daryl and Donna Breese, founders of K-9 Disc Masters, lure their German shepherd, Arasmus, into chasing the Frisbee by rolling it back and forth between them. DOUG MILHAM

Step 1. Roll or toss the Frisbee short distances and reinforce the dog for going after it and bringing it back.

Step 2. Gradually extend the distance.

Once your dog has learned to catch the Frisbee (see next section) and you are really beginning to play, you should return to shaping the chase:

Step 3. Go back to short distances and reinforce catching the tossed Frisbee.

Step 4. Extend the distance at which the dog must chase and catch.

Steps 5, 6, and more. Extend the height. Vary direction. Introduce tricky shots. Add tricks, and so on, ad infinitum.

Failure to shape the chase was, of course, a problem for those dog owners in Central Park who complained to my son that their dog leaped for the Frisbee but, when it was thrown, just stood and watched it go. Had the owners started with a one-foot toss and then gone on to a three-foot toss and, after a few days perhaps, a ten- or fifteen-foot throw, they might have gotten the desired behavior.

Shaping the chase can go hand in hand with shaping the catch, using one or more of the methods described in the next section. In fact, it is a good idea to work on several different behaviors in each training session, going from one to another as you make any progress on each one. It adds variety, reduces the danger of boredom, and keeps both you and the dog motivated. Remember, however, that you should not try to put the chase, catch, and retrieve together and expect reliable performance until some competence has been developed in each behavior separately. To rush things is to risk having your behavior chain fall apart and the dog's interest deteriorate because he does not yet really know how to win his reinforcements.

Learning to Catch

Catching an object in the air is easy for some dogs and hard for others. If it does not come naturally to your dog, you may want to shape catching as a separate skill before you ask him to try to catch a Frisbee in the air.

There are probably as many ways to achieve "catching" as there are trainers to train it. Here are a few ways:

—Toss the dog tidbits, telling him first "Catch!" and praising him for attempting to do so, and of course then for success.

—Buy some tennis balls or rubber balls of a size convenient for the dog's mouth. Bounce them in front of the dog while encouraging him to catch them on the bounce. Reinforce him at first just for making a good try and then for success.

—Enlist a friend's help: Stand about fifteen feet apart and gently bounce a small ball back and forth between you, while encouraging the dog to intercept it. Or pass a Frisbee back and forth at a temptingly low height and encourage the dog to grab it.

—Toss a tidbit or toy from hand to hand in front of the dog, playing a sort of mini keep-away yourself, and let him grab it. (This requires more coordination than some people have; it also can tempt the dog to snap at your hands and should be discontinued if that occurs.)

—Hold the dog's muzzle gently with one hand, place a tidbit on the dog's nose, and tell him to "Hold it!" Release the muzzle and tell him to catch the tidbit. At first the tidbit will just fall off, and he'll eat it off the floor. But once the dog knows what's going on, he'll learn to grab it as it falls or even to give it a toss in the air with his nose and catch it coming down. Be sure to use your conditioned reinforcer, or praise words, for successful catches.

—Wave a Frisbee over the dog's head, and when he tries to grab it, toss it just a few inches in the air so that he grabs it when it is not really in your hand. Praise him for the catch, take the Frisbee from his mouth, and repeat the action,

Anne Rathbun and her German shepherd, Mesa, play Frisbee as a relaxing change from their grueling search-and-rescue work. KAREN PRYOR

keeping the Frisbee within arm's length for quick retrieval if the dog tends to run off with it.

All of these devices, and any others you can think up, sharpen the dog's coordination and timing; they develop in him an interest in the challenge of catching a moving object. Just remember in the initial stages to reinforce every successful catch with your conditioned words and enthusiastic praise and petting. Don't assume that just eating the tidbit or getting hold of the ball or the Frisbee is sufficient reinforcement to develop the behavior.

New versus Old Skills

In all training, when working on something new, you should relax your old criteria and not expect the standards of performance in previously learned behavior that you are accustomed to getting. Sometimes the excitement of learning

something new seems to wipe out other established rules, but this is purely temporary; the old standards will be met again once the new behavior has been assimilated.

For example, suppose you have a dog who retrieves the Frisbee reliably when you roll it across the ground. Now you are working on catching it in the air. You and a friend are tossing a Frisbee back and forth to tempt the dog to grab it out of the air. If the dog *does* this, you should reinforce with your praise word for the new behavior, and ask the dog to bring the Frisbee back; but don't be surprised if he drops the Frisbee or runs off with it. Pick it up yourself or let him run around with it until he gets tired of that; you are shaping just the skillful catch at this moment. When that job is done and he is catching with some ease, you can put the catch and the retrieve back together again and just praise the retrieve.

Jumping

In addition to teaching your dog to catch objects, you may also want to shape skill in jumping or, as one sports announcer puts it, "eye-paw coordination." One way to do this is to hold the Frisbee in the air and tempt the dog to jump up for it, letting him get it now and then. You can gradually shape higher and higher jumps as the animal learns to balance and propel himself upward. Some Frisbee-dog trainers start by holding a stick and encouraging the dog to jump for it while turning and waving the stick so that the dog has to maneuver more and more. Be careful: A vertical jump in which the dog takes off from his hind legs and lands again on his hind legs puts a tremendous strain on his hip joints, an area of potential weakness. Many larger breeds tend to suffer from hip dysplasia, an inherited malformation that can be aggravated by physical stress. Small, nimble dogs are at much less risk.

To avoid any possibility of hip injury as you increase the height of your dog's jumps, move the target—stick or Frisbee—in an arc from one side to the other rather than straight up and down. This will encourage the dog to make traveling jumps in which he comes down on all fours, rather than vertical jumps that land him on his hind legs. Moving the target from side to side will also increase the dog's acrobatic skills, making his midair catches that much more spectacular.

Occasionally a dog will have a physical problem, such as a bad back, that makes jumping uncomfortable. If your dog seems reluctant to jump, trust his judgment and don't insist. Some champion Frisbee dogs don't jump at all but still play a superb game, featuring speed and tactics, catching the Frisbee close to the ground.

Frisbee Training with Young Puppies

At what age can you start Frisbee training? Since there is no arduous discipline or scolding involved, you can start at any age you like. Even a young puppy may chase a rolling

Frisbee, enjoy dragging it around, and love playing tug-of-war. Frisbee expert Don "Rocket" Hoskins described choosing a puppy from a litter of eight-week-old Australian shepherds by rolling a Frisbee past the litter. One puppy trotted after the Frisbee (which was taller than the puppy), knocked it over with a paw, seized it in his jaws, growling ferociously, and did his best to drag it back. Naturally, that pup was Don's choice for his next great Frisbee dog!

Familiarity with the Frisbee at an early age can only benefit the ultimate game. Just be sure you keep any interaction with a young puppy very brief and very cheerful. Praise and cuddle the puppy exorbitantly for anything it does right. Don't ask for more than two or three repetitions of any behavior until the pup is four or five months old. And never, never scold or show impatience about what is, after all, supposed to be a game.

Don't encourage a young puppy to jump acrobatically until it is a year old and its bones have hardened; hip and elbow injuries could result. Also, refrain from tug-of-war for a few weeks around five months of age, when the dog is losing its puppy teeth; the puppy's mouth may be sensitive, making the tussling unpleasant or painful for him.

If you have a chance to let your puppy watch older dogs playing Frisbee, by all means take advantage of it. Puppies do learn by copying their elders, and you will be amused by the intense interest the puppy takes in watching experienced Frisbee dogs and in running after them if permitted. One top trainer told me her black Labrador puppy caught its first Frisbee at three months of age by jumping completely over its mother's back to steal it.

Small Breeds

There is no reason why small dogs can't play Frisbee, and many enjoy it. When training a small dog (under fifteen inches at the shoulder), you'll find the going much easier if you obtain miniature Frisbees, three or four inches in diameter. These are available from several sources listed in the Appendix of this book. Also, you are likely to find that the dog responds better if you work from you knees or while sitting on the ground. Little dogs can be rather overwhelmed by the height of a standing person, even if it is their beloved owner. Working with short throws and a miniature Frisbee, you can have a wonderful time with even the smallest of dogs. Playing Frisbee provides great exercise for the apartment-dwelling or house-pent pet, and exercise brings all the health benefits to little dogs that it does to big ones.

Putting It All Together

When you have gone through the training tasks described in this chapter, you have trained all the elements of the Frisbee chain. The dog retrieves objects and gives them to you. He is interested in the Frisbee and will go get it if it is tossed a short distance. He is beginning to learn to catch; that is, he can catch the Frisbee when you toss it a foot or two in the air. Now you can put the whole package together and actually play Frisbee. Start with a short chase, three or four yards, and a slow, flat, predictable toss of the Frisbee. Gradually lengthen the distance over a period of five or six sessions, until the dog can get out and under the Frisbee even for long throws.

Try at first to make it easy for the dog to catch the Frisbee, ensuring some quick successes. Remember that at least half the time he needs to achieve a behavior worth reinforcing. Reinforce his catches, at whatever distance from you, by calling out "Good dog!" the instant he grabs for the Frisbee. He shouldn't have to come back and get a pat to make the connection that you like what he's doing. If the dog misses the catch, you will want him to retrieve the Frisbee anyway, of course. In this case, when he picks it up, merely call him to you; the new command reinforces the behavior of picking up the Frisbee, and you will reinforce its return each time with praise, another throw, or both. You can then save all-out

Early training: Anne rolls the Frisbee on the ground and gives lots of encouragement and praise when Mesa goes after it; Marcia Koenig and her German shepherd puppy, Orca, look on.   KAREN PRYOR

Low tosses close to the trainer come next, followed by increasingly higher tosses.   KAREN PRYOR

Letting a puppy watch an older dog play Frisbee is a good way to arouse its interest in the game.   KAREN PRYOR

Long "grounders" or rolling throws encourage Mesa to increase her distance. As a trained search-and-rescue dog, Mesa is already a reliable retriever; what she catches she will bring back.   KAREN PRYOR

"Coming back!" Anne uses short tosses into the wind to help Mesa develop skill at maneuvering under an unpredictable disc. The challenge and surprise often make the game more fun for the dog.

KAREN PRYOR

"What is this thing?" Marcia reinforces Orca's investigation with praise. KAREN PRYOR

praise (along with whistles, cheers, and applause—make it a big deal!) for actual catches.

When the dog is catching the Frisbee regularly, you can shape for more difficult catches, perhaps tilting the Frisbee as you throw it so that it curves left or right, or tipping the outside edge up so that it catches the wind and floats, hovers, or curves back toward you. All of these are fun for the dog, provided they are introduced gradually so the dog has time to develop his own skills without becoming frustrated.

You will help this final training process enormously if, from the beginning, you encourage the dog to stand beside you rather than in front of you as you prepare to throw. If the dog is facing you, he has to turn around to chase the Frisbee. Not

only does he lose valuable time but, more importantly, he is likely to lose sight of the disc as it goes sailing over his head. If he is standing beside you—on your left if you are right-handed, on your right if left-handed—and you are both facing in the same direction, he can keep his eye on the Frisbee from the moment it leaves your hand. Vary the length, style, and direction of your throws to keep your dog alert and interested, and to sharpen his skills at handling the unpredictable toss.

Try to make eye contact with your dog as often as possible. Catch his eye before you throw and as he's returning with the Frisbee. He gets both reassurance and information from this visual contact with you. It lets him know that you are, literally, focused on him and expecting a response. You may even be surprised at how much you can communicate visually. If, for example, the Frisbee suddenly changes direction and the dog loses sight of it, you can sometimes help him out by calling his name, making eye contact as he looks back, then simultaneously pointing with your whole arm and looking toward the Frisbee; the dog will often look where you are looking and thus find his target again.

Don't throw the Frisbee directly into the sun; that naturally makes it hard for the dog to see. Light-colored Frisbees are easier to keep in sight—most competition Frisbees are white—and Wham-O Manufacturing Company even makes a fluorescent Frisbee, the "Moonlighter," that can be used at twilight or under lights at night.

Finally, don't overwork your dog: When the dog gets tired, he will show it by retrieving slowly or by failing to retrieve altogether, perhaps taking the Frisbee and going to lie down in the shade. Don't force the issue if he wants to quit; save your own eagerness for another day.

Unless you are already a skilled Frisbee player, you'll find that your own throwing skills develop along with your dog's catching skills. And what a convenience it is for the novice thrower to have a dog to fetch the Frisbee! Human partners get impatient if they have to run all over the place to pick up erratically thrown Frisbees, whereas dogs are wonderfully forgiving of bad throws and make splendid learning partners.

While it is not in the province of this book to make you an expert Frisbee thrower, there are all kinds of fancy throws and tricks that can be performed with practice and to which a dog can respond. Probably the best way to become more skilled with the Frisbee is to get more accomplished Frisbee throwers to show you what they do. You can also refer to the Recommended Reading in the Appendix of this book, which lists several guides to Frisbee skills.

How long will all of this take? There's no way to tell. The founder of Frisbee-dog competition play, Alex Stein, and his champion Frisbee dog, Ashley Whippet, were invited to the White House during the Carter administration. There, on the White House lawn, Stein succeeded in teaching Amy Carter's dog, Grits, to catch a Frisbee in less than an hour. On the other hand, Mesa, the German shepherd featured in some of the pictures in this book, was a Frisbee fanatic from the age of four months, chasing and retrieving Frisbees very reliably, but not until she was eleven months old did she learn to catch the Frisbee in the air ("A big day for her and me both," says owner Anne Rathbun.)

Training your dog to play Frisbee is like any kind of training project: All you can hope for is progress. And the progress is bound to be erratic; dogs, like people, have their off-days, and so sometimes a behavior that was going well last week seems to be impossible today. As long as you are getting some overall improvement, you will eventually reach your goal. If you get discouraged, keep a notebook and write down for each training session what you worked on that day and what level of performance you were able to reinforce. Our minds play tricks on us; when we are concentrating on what still needs work, we may forget how far we have already come. A glance through the notebook will remind you of what you *have* achieved, and this in itself can be reinforcement for you.

Training by positive reinforcement will actually go faster if you avoid a timetable, a set intention to accomplish the training or any part of it within a certain time limit. Concentrate instead on making progress step by step, however long each step takes. As with any sport, you never reach perfection. There will always be new behaviors you could shape, sharper criteria and higher levels of performance to strive for, depending on your inclination. With Frisbee, however, unlike some human competitive sports, you and your dog can enjoy yourselves at any level of play and be proud of your accomplishments from the day the training starts.

CHAPTER 3

Advanced Training

Stimulus Control

One of the most important aspects of advanced training is the establishment of learned signals—signals fully understood by the animal and instantly obeyed. Psychologists call this stimulus control. It is good stimulus control that makes circus lions obey and horses impressive in dressage. In Frisbee, establishing a set of well-trained stimuli can do much to improve your dog's effectiveness and the teamwork between you. If you elect to go into competition, good stimulus control can give you a big edge over other teams.

Your dog probably already understands quite a few learned stimuli—commands such as "Sit!" and "Quiet!" and "Come here!" which he obeys some or much of the time, and words that are simply important to him, such as "dinner" and "walk" (and perhaps "Frisbee"). His understanding of these signals is probably adequate for your purposes and his, without further training. However, more formal signals, whether voice commands or hand gestures, can be of real use in advanced Frisbee skills. For example, an experienced dog often runs out the minute the Frisbee is thrown, in the direction he estimates it will go, though not actually watching the Frisbee in the air for a portion of the run. If the Frisbee is caught by the vagaries of the wind and the dog does not see it change direction, "Go right!" and "Go left!" can be useful commands. Peter Bloeme, whose dog Wizard was the 1984 national Gaines champion, has established the command "Coming back!" for times when the Frisbee reverses direction over the dog's head. The word "Jump!" can also be taught as a command should the dog tend to miss the Frisbee by not jumping for it or by jumping too late. You can establish learned signals for all kinds of tricks and stunts to dress up your Frisbee game, as well as for obedience and convenience in handling your dog.

There is a right way and a wrong way to train this kind of "on cue" behavior. Far too many dog owners try to establish stimulus control by rebuking the dog for not obeying the command, rather than praising him for obeying it correctly. This is particularly unproductive if the dog doesn't really know what the command means yet but only that he is getting yelled at again. It is far more effective to establish the behavior clearly and *then* to teach the dog that there are special benefits not just for doing the behavior but for doing it exactly when "told." The signal or word that may at first be quite meaningless to the dog thus becomes meaningful, signaling not just what behavior he is supposed to do but that a gold-plated guaranteed opportunity has arisen by which he can earn further reinforcement. Signals trained in this way, rather than by any "do what I say OR ELSE!" method, become very powerful and ensure reliable control.

Establishing a conditioned, or learned, stimulus is done by shaping one step at a time, just as you would shape a behavior. For example, if I wanted to teach my dog "Sit!" I would first elicit the behavior—perhaps by the traditional method of pulling up on the collar and pushing down on the rump—while giving the command; and I would praise the dog when it sat. I would reinforce sitting only if it followed my command, and then only if the behavior occurred promptly upon presentation of the command. I might add other criteria, step by step, such as lengthening the time in which the dog must remain sitting after a single command; or standing a little away from the dog and saying, "Sit!" and then continuing until I get a response from many yards away; or establishing a hand signal as well as a voice cue to elicit the behavior; or having the dog respond to the command in strange places or near other dogs so that he stays sitting even if I leave the room. All of these shaping steps are standard obedience exercises; none of them affects the behavior of sitting, which remains the same, but rather each one is a step in establishing good stimulus control with the command "Sit!"

People often fail to realize that a conditioned, or learned, stimulus is *not* fully established just because the dog responds to it. A dog will often seem to be responding correctly when actually the signal or cue is still very unclear in his mind. If that is the case, you may find the response breaking down under almost any kind of stress or strange circumstance. There are four points to remember when it comes to perfect control with a signal; I will continue with "Sit!" as the example.

1. The dog always sits promptly when you say "Sit!" (and you need to say it only once).

2. The dog does not sit when you do not say sit (in a

Ted Pryor giving Karen Pryor's Border terrier, Skookum, a lesson in putting behavior on cue: "Grab it!"—the cue for tug-of-war.
JON LINDBERGH

Ted gives the hand signal for keep-away.
JON LINDBERGH

"Catch it!"
JON LINDBERGH

*The second Fris-
bee signals
"Drop it!"*
JON LINDBERGH

*The hand signal
for "Drop it!"*
JON LINDBERGH

"Good boy!"
JON LINDBERGH

training or work session, that is; he should be able to do what he pleases on his own time, of course.)

3. The dog does not sit in response to some other cue such as "Lie down!"

4. The dog does not do anything else when you say "Sit!" except sit; he doesn't lie down, for instance.

You do not need to get this precise for many commands; if the dog does more or less what you want, that's fine. All obedience work, however, depends upon perfect response to commands, whether by voice or hand; in Frisbee work, the more precise the command, the more useful it will be. To get perfect stimulus control, each of the four points described above has to be established by training and may indeed have to be trained in separate shaping steps. When you are establishing commands, it is useful to keep these four points in the back of your mind and to recognize that the dog may be doing something "wrong" merely because you have not gotten that particular point across yet.

Training Some Frisbee Signals

Here is a shaping program for training "Go right!" and "Go left!" To establish these commands, tilt the Frisbee and deliberately throw an arc to the right; as the dog heads out, call his name and then say "Go right!" Simultaneously take a step to the right and move your right arm vigorously straight out sideways. The dog will glance back when he hears his name, hear the new command, and see your vigorous gesture. He may then move or look to the right on the first try, but if not, just repeat the whole thing on the next throw. After a few repetitions the dog should catch on that you are helping him find the Frisbee in the air (or on the ground, for that matter) and will begin to respond. Call out "Good dog!" the moment you see signs of responding; this is your reinforcement to him for beginning to notice the signal. If you get a clear response—the dog looks at you and moves out confidently in the right direction—make a *big* fuss over him, even going to meet him rather than waiting for him to retrieve the Frisbee.

While the dog is learning to go right on command, you must also go through the same training procedure for "Go left!"; the two commands need to be trained as if they were different behaviors. By the time you add a third directional command (such as "Behind you!" or "Coming back!") you may find the dog is learning more quickly, having now discovered that there is a class of signals that gives him directional clues. But each direction is still a different behavior. For example, sheep dog trainers find they need to use four different whistles for "left" and "right" cues: two for when the dog is headed away from the shepherd and two for when the dog is coming back. Apparently dogs don't think about left and right the same way we do.

Once the dog is responding reliably to your directional cues, you may if you wish use just the voice command. You do this by dwindling the strength of your arm and leg movements until you are not using them at all; this is called "disappearing the stimulus." If you wish to impress bystanders, you could gradually drop the voice command and also "disappear the stimulus" of the hand signal, making the gesture smaller and smaller until you are able to send your dog left or right merely with a pointed finger. Once the dog has learned a signal, he will remain attentive to it even if it is no longer a large, obvious movement. Disappearing the stimulus—until the casual observer cannot see it at all—is the basis of many circus tricks with animals and is perhaps carried to its highest perfection in the training of the Lippizaners; these dancing horses of Vienna perform all kinds of elaborate leaps and steps in accord with invisibly small motions of their riders' hands and legs.

Whenever you are establishing stimulus control, keep your signals to the dog clear and consistent. Use the same words for each object or behavior every time, and the same language to invite and encourage the dog. Of course it's still all right to chat or babytalk to your dog, should you both be just relaxing and socializing; but if you want to communicate a signal, make it a clear one. When you head outdoors to play Frisbee, for example, don't say "Let's go!" one time and "Wanna play?" another. Keep your words to the dog consistent, and the dog will soon develop a wonderful vocabulary of his own.

Whether you are training a new command or asking for a response to an old command, never give a command more than twice. Give it the first time and praise the response if you get one. (Try to give a new command such as "Left!" or "Right!" only at the moment when the dog is likely to go that way.) If you are working with the dog close to you or on the leash, give the command and then, if the dog does not respond the first time, give the command again, and gently but firmly make the dog do it: sit, get in the car, or whatever.

Bob Cox plays "merry-go-round" with his Gaines 1982 champion, Belmond. CAROLYN COX

Then praise the behavior even though you made it happen. The dog will quickly learn to respond on the first command. If you have to give a command many times or give it with threats and scolding before it is obeyed, *you* are the one who is being trained. (Incidentally, these training principles apply in precisely the same way to orders or requests to children, or adults for that matter.)

Maybe you are asking: "But why does my dog need to know 'Come,' 'Sit,' 'Stay,' 'Go left,' or any of that stuff? I just want him to play Frisbee." Sure, a dog needs to learn no more commands than you feel are necessary to make him bearable to live with. It's interesting, however, that the more new behaviors you can establish under good stimulus control—

behaviors that your dog can perform with confidence and on cue—the faster and better your dog will respond to all the things he already knows. Each new command, task, or trick he learns makes him more sophisticated or, in trainer's terms, "a sharper worker." This is the best reason I know for teaching your dog as many tasks and tricks as you have time for: It makes him a better dog.

Sometimes a command taught in one context can be very useful in another. Marcia Koenig's German shepherd, Bear, a distinguished old gentleman of eight, has been a search-and-rescue dog for many years, and ball-playing and other games of puppyhood are not very interesting to him. He is, however, an experienced and reliable retriever since retrieving is an integral part of search-and-rescue training. Bear has also been trained to obey the command "Catch!" by catching either tidbits or tossed objects. Therefore, Marcia was able to teach him Frisbee in five minutes, bypassing all the training described in this book. She took the dog out in the yard, tossed the Frisbee past him, and said "Catch!" Bear instantly understood what he was supposed to do—and knew that if Marcia asked for the behavior, she would reinforce him liberally for doing it. He took off with gusto, and the only reason the training took five minutes and several tosses was that Bear had to find out by trial and error how to get himself in the right place to make a good catch and how to hang onto the spinning disk once he'd caught it.

As Bear demonstrates, with good stimulus control you can indeed teach an old dog new tricks. It may be harder to *motivate* an old dog, especially if he has never had much agreeable experience of being trained by positive reinforcement. But if you can get him working for the payoff—be it food, fun, or approval, or all three—you can teach him anything.

How to Get Rid of Behavior You Don't Want

Even the best of dogs can exhibit undesirable behavior, and sometimes very persistently, so that *un*training a behavior that is already occurring (such as car chasing) becomes a necessity. Also, we sometimes train a dog by accident to do something we later wish he wouldn't do; we encourage the puppy to jump on the couch, for instance, and when he grows up we wish he wouldn't.

There are eight ways of getting rid of behavior you don't want. Whatever you do will be a variant of one or more of the eight methods. If you are faced with an undesirable behavior from your dog and you can't seem to get him to quit, run down the list of eight and see if some new angle suggests itself to you. I am going to go through the methods one at a time using a Frisbee-dog problem—the persistent playing of keep-away—as an example of how each method might be applied in a practical circumstance. For other problems, you might try going through the list and thinking up your own applications until you come to one that seems suitable. (For a fuller discussion of the eight methods for getting rid of behavior—in people as well as in animals see my book on reinforcement, *Don't Shoot the Dog!*)

Method 1: "Shoot the animal." Get rid of the behavior by getting rid of the dog. Not recommended in this case, although it definitely works. Give the dog away, and you will never have to watch that dog playing keep-away with you again.

Method 2: Punishment. Everybody's favorite, in spite of the fact that it never really works. If you scold the dog or catch it and spank it for playing keep-away with you, it will have even more reason to stay away from you next time.

Method 3: Negative reinforcement. A negative reinforcement is some undesirable event that can be halted or avoided by a change in behavior. In the case of keep-away, you might find that a time-out is an effective negative reinforcer: The instant the dog starts running around with the Frisbee, say "No!" and turn your back; refuse to notice the dog at all for sixty seconds. Do this every time he dodges, and the behavior may diminish rapidly.

Method 4: Extinction—letting the behavior go away by

itself. Often a puppyish tendency to play keep-away will disappear as the dog grows older or learns more about retrieving. Occasional outbursts need not be taken seriously.

Method 5: Train an incompatible behavior. Teach the dog to do something, on command and for a positive reinforcement, that he cannot accomplish and still play keep-away at the same time. "Sit!" or "Down!" would do. Once the dog is really responsive to these commands off the leash, you can use them to halt keep-away. I have trained my terrier to jump into my arms when I clap my hands; if he takes off with the Frisbee instead of dropping it, I can clap my hands and thus get the dog into my lap, and the Frisbee too. Jumping into laps is incompatible with running away.

Method 6: Put the behavior on cue. Train the dog to *play* keep-away and you play with him, with much mock chasing and excitement, whenever you give the right signal. Then give the signal less and less often. Amazingly enough, a behavior that the dog has learned to do on command will tend to occur less and less often by itself. Also *if* you have established a "Start!" signal, you can then establish a "Stop now!" signal; the dog will soon learn that when the game is over, it's over, and you can thus use the "Stop now!" cue to halt spontaneous bouts of keep-away. Notice that there is a subtle but crucial difference between forcing the dog to "Stop that!" by using threatening or angry tones, and training him to start on cue, enjoy the game, and stop on cue. The second method takes longer, but it works much more reliably. Note, too, that this is a good way to get rid of many obnoxious behaviors such as jumping up and barking too much.

Method 7: Shape the absence of the behavior: Ignore keep-away and reinforce anything and everything that is not keep-away.

Method 8: Change the motivation. This is the best method of all. If your dog loves keep-away, you need to make sure that the efforts he makes to do the things *you* want instead, such as retrieving and good catches, are liberally reinforced. Thus the dog discovers that doing the right thing, or at least taking a stab at doing the right thing, is even more fun than doing the wrong thing, and he will gradually choose to play your game instead of his own.

Canine Specialists

As dogs get good at playing Frisbee, many seem to develop favorite variations on the sport, specialties at which that dog can excel. A very fast dog, such as an Ashley Whippet, may prefer long throws and will want to race out under the Frisbee and achieve maximum-distance catches. Dr. Robert Schleser of Hawaii has a chocolate Labrador named Koa who seems determined to catch the Frisbee at the greatest height possible; thus he gets out in front of it and leaps to his full ability, taking the Frisbee at the peak of his jump. Bob Schleser points out that you would be hard put to program a computer to gauge where the Frisbee's path will intersect the dog's highest leap, but Koa calculates the feat with ease. Ted Pryor's golden retriever, Max, is a heavily built dog who quickly tires of long chases but delights in a curving toss that he can "outsmart" by taking an intersecting shortcut. For one dog, aerial acrobatics are a joy; another loves to scoop up grounders; a short-legged dog may not be much on jumping but love to show speed. It's up to you to notice what your dog likes best and does best, and then give him plenty of opportunities to work on his specialty. Animals, like people, get a thrill from operating at their peak performance level; it is always a joy to see a dog make a great catch, by the dog's own standards, and then sparkle all over with satisfaction.

Tricks and Fancy Stuff

If your dog is becoming a real crowd pleaser, you may want to add some tricks to his game. The extra training is also fun and stimulating for the dog. Here are some of the tricks the nation's top competitors use to show off their dogs' capabilities and make their demonstrations more exciting:

Over the leg: Extend your leg, plant your heel on the ground, and move the Frisbee across it so that the dog jumps over your knee to get at the Frisbee. When he does this with confidence, you can hold your leg straight out for a higher jump and throw the Frisbee for an aerial catch across your leg.

Peter Bloeme and his 1984 national champion, Wizard, a Border collie. On the command "Tap!" Wizard bunts the Frisbee back to Peter with his nose instead of catching it. KAREN PRYOR

Another competition stunt: Kato, a Labrador-setter mix, easily clears his owner, Chris Barbo, taking the Frisbee in passing.   CAROLYN COX

Daryl Breese and Arasmus demonstrating an over-the-back jump.
DOUG MILHAM

Tapping: Peter Bloeme has taught Wizard the command "Tap!" On a short throw, if Wizard hears no command, he catches the Frisbee, but if he hears "Tap!" he bumps it with his nose and knocks it back to his master, and then they can tap it back and forth between them, making a two-way game.

Over the back: Kneel on both knees with one hand on the ground and the other holding the Frisbee over your head. The aim is to get the dog to run to you, jump on your back, and take the Frisbee as he continues over your head in a flying leap. A smallish, nimble dog is required for this stunt—Border collies are fine; German shepherds are not. Wear a sturdy jacket to avoid getting scratched as the dog learns. Some trainers can do this from almost a standing position, just leaning forward a little to give the dog a bit of a platform.

Beg: Teach the dog to sit up and "beg" and/or to stand on his hind legs, and to catch the Frisbee as you toss it directly to him in these positions. Develop two voice or hand signals, one for each behavior. I use a scooping motion for "Beg!" and an extended index finger for "Stand up!" but of course any signal the dog can perceive will do once the dog has learned to associate it with the act.

Between the legs: A popular stunt is to induce the dog, by leading or "targeting" him with the hand-held Frisbee, to run between your legs from back to front; then you reinforce him by throwing the Frisbee as he passes through. The end result is a dog that makes a catch, comes running back, drops the Frisbee in front of you, and then runs round behind you and dashes through your legs to chase the next throw.

Acrobatics: People love to see dogs flip around in the air after the Frisbee. Perhaps the king of all "acrobatic" dogs is Bill Murphy's many-time champion Brutus, also known as Bouncing Boo. The picture on page 64 is a routine catch for this dog. Don't try to force your dog to make twisting catches and somersaults if acrobatics don't come naturally to him. Some dogs "know where the ground is" and always land on their feet, while others fall and can easily get hurt. If you do have a fancy diver by nature, you can encourage twists by having the dog sit about twenty feet away facing you and by teaching him to catch the Frisbee from a standing start in that position. Then toss the Frisbee just a foot or two to the dog's right or left so that the dog has to put some torque in his jump. This will help him learn to twist in the air and still land securely. You can then try longer throws with crooked or unpredictable trajectories, to encourage the dog to turn in the air.

Rollers and sliders: To give the dog something new to do, throw the Frisbee so that it rolls along the ground or slides a few inches above the ground. You can also throw the Frisbee

The 1980 national champion, Kona, competing at halftime before a football crowd in the Rose Bowl, catches and holds four Frisbees at once. IRV LANDER ASSOCIATES

at a downward angle so that it hits the ground and skips up, challenging the dog to catch it off the bounce. Skilled throwers can even skip the Frisbee twice.

Distance: Perhaps the most dramatic and difficult feat in the Frisbee-dog repertoire is the long-distance catch. "Rocket" Hoskins' 1983 distance champion, Bingo, won with a catch of 107 yards, the length of a football field and then some. To go that distance the Frisbee may be traveling as fast as fifty miles an hour and spinning at 100 revolutions a minute. The dog needs a head start and a lot of determination. The person needs skill in throwing. Interestingly, long, long throws depend less on power than on correct form and timing; see the Recommended Reading list in the Appendix of this book for expert advice on throwing form and techniques.

Multiples: One popular exhibition or competition technique is to throw the dog several Frisbees at once. Each one leaves the thrower's hand as the dog is heading for or about to catch the previous one. The effect is a series of leaps and catches, one right after the other, each one difficult and exciting. Bob Inga, owner of regional champion Noogies, likes to throw multiples around himself: one in front, one to the left, one behind, and one to the right. In addition to the spectacular leaps and catches Noogies specializes in, to get to the next Frisbee in time she must streak at top speed in a hundred-foot circle around her owner, adding to the drama of the display. Another technique is to send the dog out on a long catch and then throw multiples—first to the left, then to the right, then left and right again—so that the dog has to zigzag madly to catch each one. Again, the multiples show off the dog's speed and agility.

To catch multiple tosses the dog needs to learn to drop the Frisbee he has just caught rather than retrieve it, if and when he sees another one coming at him. It is important to

"Multiples": Catching and dropping five Frisbees in rapid succession extends the dog to his utmost. Pepper Schwartz and his mixed-breed retriever, Chino, are top national competitors. CAROLYN COX

establish some kind of verbal command to notify the dog when one is switching from single to multiple catches. While the dog will learn to watch for the next Frisbee in the air, he may not always see it, and a verbal command will at least warn him to look. "Comin' at you!" or "One more time!" are phrases some trainers use. It doesn't matter what phrase you choose as long as you are consistent and always use the same words. Also, dogs who learn to catch multiples but do not

know any clear command for when the multiples are coming sometimes take to dropping the Frisbee as soon as they catch it, even when you are not throwing multiples and the dog should be bringing it back.

To throw multiples, carry a stack of three to six extra Frisbees in your nonthrowing arm. When they have all been thrown, caught, and dropped, you pick them up yourself.

The number of stunts and special behaviors one can establish with the Frisbee or weave into the Frisbee game is

Personal style: Skilled Frisbee dogs tend to develop their own specialties. Bill Murphy's Brutus, also known as Bouncing Boo, goes in for acrobatics. CHICAGO SUN-TIMES/RICH HEIN

probably endless. One competitor starts his routine by making his dog lie down; he then lies down beside the dog, and they both roll over. You can train the dog to bring you a beer or to bark when you mention your favorite ball team. The dog can leap into your arms on command or through your arms held in a circle. You can train him to balance the Frisbee on his nose, put the Frisbee in the lap of anyone you point out, or flip it upside down or right side up in his mouth. Tricks and stunts are limited only by the ingenuity of the trainer. The hardest part is thinking them up. The experienced trainer can usually duplicate anything he sees another trainer do; if you come up with something new, you can bet others will pick it up—that's why circus acts seem so similar. So if you and your dog like doing tricks and other people copy you, don't be discouraged. Just sharpen your imagination. You may come up with something new that's much better than anything that's been described here. This is a young sport, and the fun has just begun.

Your Dog, the Athlete: Avoiding Injuries

When you ask your dog to catch Frisbees in midair and on the run, you are asking for top-level athletic performance. As in any athletic performance, the possibility of injury does exist.

Muscles and Joints: Strains and Sprains

As your dog becomes a better Frisbee player, you may notice an increase in muscular development, especially in the upper muscles of the legs. Top competition dogs have hard, well-defined muscles, like Olympic divers and for the same reason: they must become acrobats as well as athletes, able to jump, twist, and tumble with great control.

In developing this kind of physique in your dog you should take the same commonsense precautions that you would take with your own body. Warm up the dog with a little light work—a five-minute walk, a few short tosses—before he begins going after those high catches or long powerhouse throws. This is especially important if the dog has been inactive, sitting in the car or lying around the house all day. Use common sense during your training or play sessions, and stop before the dog is overtired. The dog will usually quit playing before he gets totally worn out, but if he is very enthusiastic, you may have to think about stopping for him.

Develop your dog's stamina gradually just as you would in your own athletic conditioning. You might want to push him a little harder each week of practice, staying out a little longer and throwing a few more times than you were doing the week before. But don't ask your dog to work routinely for ten minutes a day and then suddenly expect him to perform for half an hour.

Remember that dogs get stiff and sore just as we do, especially when they have done more than they are used to. If you do have an unusually strenuous day's session, rest the dog the next day or two, with easy tosses or light exercise, before going back to full speed. He can't tell you if he's stiff, but you can judge it by watching, especially the first few minutes. His condition will improve more rapidly if he is not worked beyond his capacity.

At the end of a hard romp with the Frisbee, give your dog a chance to cool off, perhaps by walking him on the leash, if there is no place to let him just walk by himself, before you coop him up indoors again.

All of these precautions help to protect the dog against strains and sprains, but the best protection against muscle injury is a well-conditioned musculature combined with proper warming up and cooling down.

A look at the photographs in this book will make it clear that dogs playing Frisbee often jump high enough to put great strain on their leg joints in landing. Most dogs learn to land safely, even after twisting and turning in midair in all kinds of weird ways, but if you hear your dog yelp upon landing, you should immediately assume that he has wrenched something. Stop playing, give him a rest for two or three days, and watch carefully for signs of soreness.

One way to protect high-leaping dogs against these reentry injuries is to throw the Frisbee to one side of the dog or the other, rather than in a line directly over the dog's head. This gives the dog a chance to land on all four feet or at least to catch himself with his forepaws. Since some breeds (German shepherds and collies, among others) have a genetic tendency to hip dysplasia, a congenital weakness, and also hip joint arthritis, one should be especially careful to develop in these dogs a horizontal or flying leap rather than to encourage them to jump straight up.

Unexpected or uncertain footing can lead to injuries in any athlete, dog or human. Play Frisbee with your dog on flat ground, not near banks or gullies or knolls. Never ask him to catch the Frisbee on asphalt or pavement. Go slowly if you must play on an artificial surface, such as Astroturf; like humans, some dogs love it and others can't seem to stop slipping and sliding.

Finally, if you have a great leaper, you may want to resist the temptation to let a friend toss the Frisbee. Everybody wants to be the one to throw the disc to a super jumper; but everybody throws a little differently, and your dog is used to your throws. A bad throw or just a different throw may be enough to bring the dog down awkwardly or off-balance so

Few dogs get as acrobatic as the many-times champion Bouncing Boo, here descending on the Frisbee from above. But any dog who loves to jump should be watched carefully for strains and sprains, and played with only on flat ground and safe footing. CAROLYN COX

that he hurts himself. More than one competition dog has been sidelined with a strained paw or sore hip because his owner allowed a friend to throw the Frisbee to him "just once." I don't mean you can never share the fun of playing Fisbee with your dog, just that you should be aware of the potential problem, especially with a very high jumper, and advise any other thrower to use caution and common sense.

Tooth and Mouth Injuries

One common injury casued by the Frisbee is tooth abrasion. A dog who has been playing a lot of Frisbee for two or three years or more may have had his lower canines worn down to half their normal length. This doesn't seem to cause dogs any discomfort nor is it unsightly, so usually it's nothing to worry about. But once in a great while the whirling Frisbee will knock a tooth loose, usually an upper canine; you should think of this immediately if your dog drops the disc and paws at his face, or if there is bleeding around the front teeth. A loosened tooth does cause pain and can lead to infection, and a missing canine is noticeable (and will disqualify your dog from the purebred show ring, if that is a consideration for you). Take the dog to your veterinarian. A loosened tooth will usually reset itself if the dog is given a rest and is fed on soft food for a few days.

Nicks and cuts inside the mouth are also common Frisbee-dog injuries. Any time a dog's tooth happens to pierce the Frisbee, it raises a little triangular flap of plastic that may be quite sharp. Almost always the disc is spinning when the dog catches the Frisbee—that is what keeps it airborne—and on a long toss it may be spinning very hard. Thus each little spike of plastic on the Frisbee surface has a chance of whirling through the dog's mouth and cutting him. Since most dogs catch the Frisbee with their whole jaw, using the back teeth as well as the front to trap the moving disc, these cuts and scratches will usually occur at the back corners of the dog's jaws behind the teeth, on the roof of the mouth, or in the corners of the lips. If the thrower is left-handed and spins the disc counterclockwise, the dog will get more cuts on the left side of its mouth; if the thrower is right-handed, the cuts will appear on the right side.

A few nicks probably won't bother the dog much. One tournament competitor told me he uses Ambesol or some other drugstore oral anesthetic on the dog's mouth cuts. The best preventive, of course, is to keep your Frisbee in good condition. Use a file or some sandpaper on obvious rough spots on the inside of the Frisbee (where the dog's tongue can get cut) as well as the outside. A throwing Frisbee that has more than a few nicks and tears in it should be gotten rid of or turned into a chewing toy.

A "chomper." Some dogs bite the Frisbee hard, and others have soft mouths and take hold lightly; the difference is inborn and cannot be altered by training. KAREN PRYOR

Some dogs catch the Frisbee gently, with what bird dog trainers call a "soft mouth"; others chomp down on it hard and often bite right through. Bird dog trainers have methods for trying to deal with this; one of the more gruesome is to teach the dog to fetch a stick and then wrap the stick in barbed wire. But most of the Frisbee-dog trainers I've talked to seem to feel that the difference is inborn and cannot readily be modified by training. If you have a chomper, you will probably have to resign yourself to going through a lot of Frisbees in a year. You could buy especially tough Frisbees that hold up a bit longer (as offered by one firm; see Appendix). Another solution would be to buy inexpensive Frisbees in quantity and dispose of them frequently, before ragged edges cut up the dog's mouth.

Occasionally a dog is actually allergic to plastic: the dog may develop swollen and painful lips and gums, and an ugly rash on the nose, from repeated contact with the Frisbee.

(The same thing can happen to allergic dogs who drink from a plastic water bowl.) If your vet diagnoses an allergy to plastic you might want to try a different type of disc (again, see Appendix for sources).

Finally, dogs who like to catch grounders run the risk of wearing all the hair off their chins. If you begin to notice this condition, simply cut back on the grounders you throw.

Other Cuts and Abrasions

Dogs running over rough ground can get cuts in or between the pawpads; these are painful and slow to heal, so be careful not to play with your dog in areas where you see broken glass, tin cans, or metal, or in high grass that may hide dangerous debris.

Some dogs are born with dewclaws, little extra toes on the inside of the lower legs, just above the paws. The purebred standards of some breeds—Newfoundlands, Saint Bernards, and all retrievers—require dewclaws, which are thought to be of assistance on slippery footing. In others, the dewclaws are not important or are customarily removed while the puppy is tiny. Presumably a Frisbee dog with dewclaws on the front legs may gain some traction from this extra toe in fast sliding turns, but occasionally the dewclaw catches on the ground and partly rips off, making a very nasty tear up the dog's leg. If your dog has prominent dewclaws and also plays a sliding, skidding game, you may want to discuss with your vet the possibility of removing the dewclaws to prevent this accident. If a dewclaw is torn even a little, you should take the dog to the vet immediately. Dewclaw injuries bleed a lot, cause pain, and need treatment.

Heat Prostration

This is a killer. Dogs have difficulty venting heat because they have few sweat glands and primarily must pant to cool themselves by evaporation. So the intense activity of Frisbee-playing can induce heat exhaustion, especially in hot weather. If you are playing on the beach or on a very hot day, be alert to prevent overheating. Offer your dog water frequently (a Frisbee makes a good water dish). Rest your dog in the shade. Pour water over his back and head if he seems uncomfortably hot. Some Frisbee-dog clubs take a toddler's plastic wading pool to the park when they get together on summer days; they fill it with water so the dogs can get a drink easily and stand or lie down in the water to cool off after a hard workout.

The danger signs of heat prostration are weakness, listlessness, a glazed look in the eyes, and sharp, hard panting that the dog can't seem to stop. If these occur, before you give the dog water to drink, cool him by sponging water over him or by standing him in water (the paws ventilate heat well). Heavy-coated dogs naturally feel the heat more; as a precaution you might consider clipping the coat to keep your shaggy dog athlete more comfortable in summer.

The commonest cause of heat prostration mortality in dogs is being shut in a car in the hot sun. Temperatures can become intolerable in just a few minutes. Be careful not to add the stress of a hot car to the heating caused by a strenuous workout on a hot day.

CHAPTER *5*

Frisbee Dogs: Breeds and Types

I am always amazed at psychologists and others who argue that all or most behavior is learned, not inborn. One has only to look at the many breeds of dogs and the variety of behavioral traits to realize that a good part of mammalian behavior is genetically controlled. Each breed of dog was developed not just to look a certain way but to behave in a certain way. Shepherd breeds herd and guard sheep and cattle; pointers and setters range widely, while spaniels stay closer to the hunter. Terriers (from the French *terre*, meaning earth) have a strong tendency to dig, having been bred to go after small prey in holes, and boxers and bulldogs grab and hang on, having been bred originally as guard dogs and fighters. Sometimes the "behavior blueprint" bred by humans into the dog is very specific: Most dogs leap over an obstacle or down a short drop with their front legs forward and their hind legs tucked up behind, as horses leap; but Labrador retrievers, even from early puppyhood, tend to leap with all four legs thrust forward, landing with a thump—the "ice breaker" leap designed to enable them to plunge through frozen marshes when retrieving ducks in winter, a very specific bit of selective breeding for behavior.

Using reinforcement training techniques one can train any animal to do anything it is physically and mentally capable of doing. But because of inbred behavioral as well as physical characteristics, some dogs are much less likely than others to be "naturals" at the Frisbee game. There are dogs who can't catch the Frisbee because they can't see it—Old English sheep dogs, for example, which often have too much hair in their eyes to see well. Other breeds, such as some of the hounds, use their noses so much more than their eyes that they just don't seem to register moving objects as being of importance, even though they seem to see fairly well. Most terriers will chase a rolling or tossed Frisbee with gusto and grab it up; but terriers are bred to hang onto small prey with ferocious tenacity and typically want to shake the Frisbee to death rather than give it up for another throw.

Very large breeds, such as Great Danes and New-foundlands, have trouble getting off the ground to make aerial catches and may be subject to hip problems, which can be aggravated by jumping or by quick stops and turns. Small-mouthed breeds, including most of the toys, may have trouble catching even a miniature Frisbee because their jaws are too weak to hang onto it as it spins. Some breeds are physically hampered by structural handicaps, such as pushed-in noses that restrict breathing (pugs and English bulldogs) or ex-tremely heavy coats (chows and spitzes) that lead to overheat-ing. Short-legged breeds such as dachshunds may have trouble running fast enough to get under a Frisbee. And finally, some breeds—Scotties come to mind—are such independent souls that they would rather play their own games than cooperate in yours.

However, with good training and a willing dog, even the most unlikely specimens may become great Frisbee enthusiasts. The television show "That's Incredible!" has featured a Chihuahua that plays brilliantly with a miniature Frisbee, and Donna Breese's very successful competition dog, Yote, shown on page 16, is half-coyote. The first and most famous national champion, Ashley Whippet, is, of course, a whippet, a small and dainty breed; it is not a natural retriever but a breed with incredible speed, determination, and the ability to leap like Rudolph Nureyev.

The principal assets of most Frisbee dogs are long legs, strong jaws, and some natural tendency to retrieve. The legs get them out there and up in the air, the jaws help them to hang on to the furiously spinning disc, and the inbred tendency to bring the prey back makes the training easier. You can make a lot of training mistakes and still get good results with a Labrador, golden retriever, spaniel, poodle (originally a duck-retrieving breed), or mixed breed with some retriever in it.

All dogs—and retrievers are no exception—love to play "keep-away" and to race around in circles daring you to try to grab the Frisbee as they pass. Perhaps the easiest way to get around this problem is to start with a dog that is also endowed with an inbred tendency to obey commands, such as German shepherds or other working breeds—the breeds considered suitable for obedience training, search-and-rescue, seeing-eye work, and similar complex trained tasks.

These highly trainable breeds usually love to play Frisbee and learn it readily. Since 1976, when the first Frisbee-dog tournaments were established, many of the serious competitors have narrowed their choices down to two working breeds: Border collies and Australian shepherds, or "heelers" (so-called because they nip the heels of cattle to make them move). The Border collie, bred on the border between England and Scotland, is not the large, long-haired, "Lassie" type collie but a middle-sized, unpretentious black and white dog, often with pale or blue eyes, bred for herding sheep. The Australian shepherd, which comes in various sizes, is a shaggy, bluish or reddish and white dog sometimes vaguely resembling a bushy collie. Both breeds are nimble and active, with strong jaws suitable for biting recalcitrant cattle or sheep. Both of them are indefatigable herders; in fact, they are almost too zealous. Friends of mine who bought a Border collie for a house dog finally had to give it away because it kept herding their three small children into a corner of the yard and holding them there; and some heelers have a lamentable tendency to nip the heels not only of cattle but of running children. But the major quality these two breeds share, and the one that in my opinion differentiates them from most other breeds, is their aggressive inbred desire to work, and consequently a readiness to learn and obey commands. Animal behaviorist J. P. Scott of the University of Maine demonstrated that Border collies are so preprogrammed to obey orders that you can put a dish of food next to a six-week-old Border puppy, and say "No!" and leave the room, and the puppy will not touch the food.

At the jobs they were bred for, both breeds are pros: They will work until they drop, risk bodily harm and court exhaustion routinely, work without supervision, learn and obey dozens of commands, and be satisfied by the meagerest of reinforcements. Their reward seems to be intrinsic in the mere opportunity to do what they are so strongly programmed to do—fast, tricky work on command.

The result is that while other breeds may like or even love playing Frisbee, herders take it seriously. This is life's major endeavor. A Border collie or an "Aussie" may misbehave like any other dog in normal life—chew the furniture, pick fights with other dogs, lunge and pull on the leash, and ignore reprimands—but when it comes to Frisbee, these dogs become glittery-eyed, fanatic perfectionists. They will do *anything* to make a great catch.

So at present the pros are picking promising pups from

these breeds. Some of the all-time-great Frisbee dogs, however, have been crossbred, like Bob Inga's regional champion Noogies, a half-whippet, half–golden retriever, or out-and-out mutts like Kansas geologist Pepper Nichols' regional champion Chino, a leggy yellow dog with some retriever and some other unknown ancestors. Many a dog doomed to die in the pound owes its life to some Frisbee player who saw in it a promising build and a courageous disposition, the marks of a possible Frisbee dog.

It's my own suspicion that the great Frisbee dogs of the future could be a new breed developed with special behavioral traits for the demands of the sport. There are a number of precedents. For example, a new breed of sheepherding dog has recently been developed in New Zealand, where vast terrains make the close-working Border collie ineffective. Called the "huntaway," this working dog has built-in behavior just the opposite of the usual sheep dog's. It is a barker, rather than a silent stalker; it chases the sheep away from its master, not back to him; it works at a gallop, not at the cautious "keep 'em calm but moving" crawl of the Border collie; and it can push a thousand sheep through a gate a mile away in twenty minutes. This dog was developed by crossing the obedient, fanatically hardworking Border collie with the Gordon setter, to get the legs and distance-covering movement; with cattle dogs such as heelers and briards to add the barking and push; and with anything else someone thought might be useful. The dogs look like anything and everything (breeding for looks is beneath a real huntaway fancier), but in a few short generations the behavior has been most impressively hard-wired in.

The ideal Frisbee dog, then, could be developed the same way. It will have speed, grace, powerful jaws, great eyesight, agility, energy, and a fanatic desire to get the job done. Frisbee expert Don "Rocket" Hoskins (who himself uses Australian shepherds for his Frisbee-dog demonstrations) suggests a cross between a greyhound and a pitbull: If such a dog got mad at you, you sure wouldn't want to be on the same side of a fence with it, but could that dog catch Frisbees!

Picking Out a Frisbee Puppy

If you are going to acquire a puppy with the intent of making it into a Frisbee dog, the foregoing information will suggest what breed or mix of breeds might make for a good prospect. However, the disposition of the individual dog will also determine not only how it plays Frisbee but whether you can stand to live with the beast. Fortunately, there now exists a way to gauge that disposition.

Dog psychologists have discovered that certain aspects of a dog's adult personality, especially its natural degree of dominance or submissiveness, can be determined as early as eight weeks of age and will remain an important factor in the dog's behavior and responsiveness to training all its life, whether it is male or female, a large or small breed, a working dog, hunting dog, or mutt. For example, if you put any puppy on its back and restrain it gently for thirty seconds, some will cry and even urinate in fear, some will lie quietly, some will struggle and then try to play or lick your hand, and others, very dominant by nature, will struggle violently and ceaselessly and even try to bite. Encouraging a puppy to follow after you also reveals its temperament: The submissive dog may show fear, the average dog will follow with tail up, the very dominant pup will run between your legs and trip you, and the highly independent dog (probably *not* a good Frisbee prospect) won't follow at all. Make a loud noise near pups (bang a pan or slam a car door), and you may see both the very submissive and the very assertive pups react strongly, while other pups merely evince curiosity.

Which end of the scale you will enjoy most depends on your own temperament and situation; all may be fine dogs, but not for all families. For example, you might not want a very dominant dog nor a very submissive one around small children. A top Frisbee prospect should be dominant rather than overly submissive, but not so dominant or independent that it will be difficult to train. Dog psychologist William Campbell has developed a simple puppy selection test that will help you to choose the particular puppy in a litter who will fit into your family and give you the kind of response you want. Dr. Campbell's "Behavior Rx for Selecting a Puppy" is available through veterinarians or from his offices in Oregon (see Recommended Reading in the Appendix). I know of no better guarantee that you will be happy with your dog than to make one or more of Dr. Campbell's tests before choosing the pup.

CHAPTER *6*

Clubs and Competitions

The Gaines Ashley Whippet Invitationals

Formal Frisbee-dog competition really began with a dog named Ashley Whippet and a daring move by his owner, Alex Stein. From puppyhood the dog was a fanatic Frisbee player, and by three years of age he had become truly phenomenal, drawing crowds wherever he and Alex worked out together. Whippets are small dogs, bred for racing, and Ashley could travel up to thirty miles an hour, could get out and under a Frisbee thrown the length of a football field (100 yards or more), and could leap and take a disc out of the air nine feet off the ground.

Looking for exposure for his performer, Alex went to Hollywood but got nowhere with the agents and talent scouts. So, as reporter Douglas Kirk has described it, "On a hot

August night at Dodger Stadium, at the bottom of the eighth inning in a nationally televised game between the Dodgers and the Cincinnati Reds, Ashley Whippet and Alex Stein slipped out onto the field and started their routine. 'We were either going to burst upon the scene or that would be it,' says Stein. At one point during the eight minutes they were out on the field, Reds center fielder Jim Wynn threw down his glove and exclaimed, 'That dog can catch better than I can!' By the time the security guards escorted Stein from the field, the crowd of fifty thousand was on its feet, cheering and screaming for more. Ashley was a hit."

Ashley's debut was almost his demise; while Alex went to jail, the dog disappeared for three anxious days. As it turned out, the bewildered little dog had been rescued and cared for by a family at the ball game, and it took them three days to locate Alex and reunite him with Ashley. At this point another benefactor materialized—Irv Lander, a California sports promoter, and dog lover. He, with Alex, found a sponsor, Gaines dog food, devised a program of training and competition for disc-catching dogs and their owners, and started a new American sport—Frisbee-dog tournaments.

The first national tournament was held in 1976. By 1984 the competitions had been officially titled the Gaines Ashley Whippet Invitationals and included nearly a hundred and fifty local and state meets, eight United States regional competitions, and a grand World Finals at Comiskey Park in Chicago, prior to a Chicago White Sox game. The local competitions are usually held in public parks and are organized and supervised by Parks Department recreation officials, the Humane Society, or local veterinarians. Anyone may participate, and anyone may go to the regional competitions, regardless of whether or not he won or scored in the local trials.

Regional finals are often held in a stadium in association with a football or baseball game, in this way providing the dogs and owners with an enthusiastic crowd and the crowd with an amusing show. In 1984, for example, the Texas regional finals were held in the Houston Astrodome before a

Competition requires training in teamwork. Here Chris Barbo and Kato compete at Comiskey Park, Chicago, during the 1984 Gaines national finals. CAROLYN COX

Houston Astros game. Only the national finals are truly invitational in that they are restricted to the eight regional winners (more if there are regional ties) and one or two exhibition dogs. (At the 1984 finals Ashley Whippet, twelve years old, retired but still present, quivered at the end of his leash whenever a Frisbee flew by; his sons and daughters replaced him, putting on long-distance demonstrations and high-catch displays.) For the annual finals, Gaines pays all the finalists' travel expenses and gives the winners U.S. Savings Bonds; Irv Lander and Alex Stein locate the hotel that will put up with a dozen visiting dogs, supervise the contest, and look after all the participants.

The nature of the competition has varied somewhat from year to year, but in general there is some kind of fixed competition in which the owner must stand in one location, either within a circle or behind a line, and throw the Frisbee a

Alex Stein, owner and trainer of the first great competition Frisbee dog, Ashley Whippet, with Ashley (lower left) and three of the dog's descendants. WALT MANCINI

minimum distance, while the dog catches and returns it; the aim is to make as many catches and returns as possible, using a single disc, within a one-minute period. Then a second type of competition is held, generally called Freeflight in which the owner and dog may run all over the field if they wish, use up to five Frisbees, and do anything they can think up, being judged on showmanship and teamwork as well as the dog's leaping ability and the degree of difficulty of the catch. Here the competitors show off their dogs' ability to catch several Frisbees at once or in quick succession; to leap over their owners; to do tricks, tumbles, and acrobatics; and to make their most spectacular catches. Some routines are literally choreographed and set to music; I've seen one dog dressed in a red bandanna and wristbands, to match his owner's red socks. Anything goes.

Above all, however, it's athletic performance and superior training that count. And the training, of animal and of self, does not come easily; it is the result of long practice, lots of positive attention to the dog, and lots of self-discipline for the owner. Lander and Stein are justly proud of the high level of good sportsmanship among their competitors and of the beneficial effects of this kind of sports experience on young competitors. National-level competitors I've met have ranged from professional men in their thirties to laborers, policemen, housewives, and college and high school students—all with a common interest, of course, but all, also, with a common outlook: the camaraderie of the positive reinforcement trainer. People may take their competition very seriously and drive hundreds of miles routinely to practice and compete, but there are no training "secrets" and few rivalries. Everyone shares training ideas and devices because everyone knows that it's not what you do but how you do it that gets results.

As the seconds tick away, Tony Frediani and his Australian heeler, Duke, get in one last good catch for Judge Alex Stein during the semifinals of the 1984 Gaines championship competition.
CAROLYN COX

For information about Ashley Whippet Invitationals in your area, write:

Ashley Whippet Invitational Headquarters
P. O. Box 1683
Encino, CA 91426

or call their toll-free number: 1-800-423-3268 (in California, 818-780-4915).

K-9 Disc Masters

As the numbers of Frisbee competitors increased in the late seventies, many felt the need for an organization that would bring them together outside of the Gaines tournaments held in the summer and fall. Some of the top competitors wanted more activities and work for their highly trained dogs, and some wanted to get away from the commercial sponsorship and the inevitable restraints and formalization of activities that sponsorship must impose. K-9 Disc Masters was the result, a club run entirely by volunteers. It started in 1980 and now has seven regional directors, competitions, informal meets, and regional and national finals, and it publishes a quarterly newsletter. Many of the members also participate in the Gaines tournaments; the mood seems to be one not of rivalry but of extending the sport and the opportunities for players.

A major activity of K-9 Disc Masters consists of organizing halftime entertainment with Frisbee dogs and owners at college and pro football games. Six dogs and owners on the field at once, performing a planned series of stunts, is a guaranteed crowd pleaser; and the gang usually ends the show by sailing dozens of Frisbees right into the audience. The California K-9 Disc Masters, who perform at the Rose Bowl, at Candlestick Park, and elsewhere in the state, often have more invitations to perform than they can handle. In other parts of the country, K-9 Disc Master members put on shows for schools, retirement homes, and charity events.

Proud and happy: Frank Allen and his dog, Kona, 1980 national champion. A joyful partnership with an animal is the great bonus in canine Frisbee. IRV LANDER ASSOCIATES

Membership in K-9 Disc Masters is open to anyone, costs $10 a year, and includes a newsletter full of training tips and discounts on supplies. Write to:

> K-9 Disc Masters
> Route 4, Box 455C
> Bakersfield, CA 93309

For names of regional directors and clubs, information about Frisbee-dog halftime shows or other performances, or any other information, contact the national coordinator, Daryl Breese, at the above address, or phone 805-589-3375.

The Last Word

Frisbee Cats

Impossible? Not at all. All cats chase moving objects; the Frisbee is a moving object. Many cats catch birds or try to. Cats can catch Frisbees in the air exactly the way they try to catch any flying object: They leap up and grab it with their paws, and then put it in their mouths. To get your cat to catch a Frisbee, all you need are some mini Frisbees (see source list at the back of the book) and a cat. Start with rollers: Encourage the cat to bat and play with the Frisbee, then sail a few fliers gently past the cat's nose, and you may have a

Frisbee-catching cat with almost no training at all. In fact, cats being the hard-wired, preprogrammed hunting creatures that they are, you may elicit something else quite interesting: the innate "bird-catching" sound of the cat, a sort of "k-k-k-k-k-k" made with the mouth open, that cats make in no other circumstance save when hunting flying prey. (It has the function, I have observed, of making all other cats and kittens within hearing crouch motionless and look where the hunter is looking.)

This is a lot of fun for the cat, and I'm sure we cat lovers would all rather have our pets catching Frisbees for fun than catching wildlife. However, what about the retrieving part of the game? Do cats do that?

Some cats are natural retrievers; Siamese and Burmese cats seem particularly inclined to play fetch, but many others will do it too. The classic cat-retrieve toy is a crumpled piece of tinfoil or cellophane—a cigarette pack wrapper is traditional—and many an apartment cat will chase and bring back a thrown toy of this sort over and over until the owner gets tired of the game. I once had a Burmese cat who retrieved pencils; she often initiated the game by finding a pencil and carrying it to me, for me to then throw and her to chase—usually when I had been writing at the typewriter all morning, and she was bored.

If you have a cat who retrieves, all you really have to do to play Frisbee is learn to throw a mini Frisbee so that it hovers and floats (and they are easier to hover than the big ones), and then introduce your cat to this great new toy, encouraging him with coaxing talk to bring it back. The opportunity for another chase and catch is the reinforcement for the retrieve, just as it is with dogs. Stop the game the minute the cat seems to lose interest—or a little bit sooner, if possible. Cats get bored quickly.

If your cat does not retrieve and shows no interest in the Frisbee, you can shape the behaviors of batting at the Frisbee, chasing rollers, and picking up the Frisbee—all of which will lead to the Frisbee game—by using food reinforcement and a step-by-step shaping program. Cats cannot be trained easily by force, as dogs can, but most cats will learn behaviors very quickly for a conditioned reinforcer followed by some preferred food. Most cast are suckers for diced ham or cheese; I often use these food rewards to teach little tricks to other people's cats, just to show it can be done. The San Diego Wild Animal Park in California has featured a marvelous show of trained house cats. The trainers, using a "cricket," a child's clicker toy, to notify the cat when it does the desired thing, have shaped tightrope walking, balancing feats, pole climbs, and so on. They follow each behavior with the sound of the cricket and at the end of the behavior chain offer a food reward. The professionals can do just about anything with cats, using food, and so can you. (For complete instructions on designing behavioral shaping programs with cats, people, or any other subject, see my book *Don't Shoot the Dog!* which is listed under Recommended Reading.)

The Useful Frisbee Dog

In closing, here are a few practical uses of the Frisbee with your Frisbee-trained dog.

Once the Frisbee has become a favored object, you can use it for training other behavior. For example, in training a dog to sit and stay at a distance from the owner—or in a strange place or with the owner out of sight, as is done in advanced obedience work—you can sometimes reassure the dog in early training stages by leaving the Frisbee next to him. The dog is already trained to sit still, so he won't play with the Frisbee but instead will feel that he is guarding his possession, which helps to take his mind off the anxiety of being left alone in the first place. If you have a dog who barks or cries when you leave it alone in the car, you may be able to reduce this behavior in the same way by producing the Frisbee and putting it next to the dog as you get out of the car.

Search-and-rescue dogs are trained to locate missing persons by air-scenting. In the early stages of training, one way of motivating the dog to go find somebody he doesn't know is to let the dog see that person go away out of sight—carrying the dog's beloved Frisbee! The dog thus has a strong interest in finding out where that person has gone.

We've considered the value of the Frisbee as a dog exerciser when the person does not wish to exercise. Indiana State Trooper Bob Cox, owner of 1981 Gaines national champion Belmond, carries this one step further. When it's snowing and 40 below outside, he opens the kitchen door, throws the Frisbee fifty yards or so, closes the door on the rapidly exiting dog, then sits down until he hears a paw on the door; he opens it, takes the Frisbee from the dog's mouth, sails it away again, closes the door, and thus keeps his dog happily worn out without having to do so much as put on a mitten himself.

Once trained, a Frisbee dog can be a great play experience for the retarded or handicapped, catching and fetching any kind of toss they can make. Taking the family dog outside to play Frisbee is a fine way to get noisy kids out of the house. Provided you have a long corridor or basement or play room free of fragile objects, indoor fun with a soft Frisbee (see Equipment Sources in the Appendix) or mini Frisbee can occupy dogs and children alike when cooped up because of bad weather or a cold. And if you are single, I don't need to tell you what a great asset your Frisbee dog can be in meeting people.

But mostly, as one expert puts it, Frisbee training is quality time with your dog. The fun and companionship you both get out of it can make it one of the memorable experiences of a lifetime.

Appendix

Recommended Reading

BOOKS

Don't Shoot the Dog! by Karen Pryor. Simon and Schuster, 1984; Bantam Books, 1985. $13.95, or $4.95 in paperback.

A complete guide to operant conditioning and reinforcement, written in everyday language, for use by parents, pet owners, coaches, bosses, and trainers of all kinds. This is mostly about people, not dogs, but it's the only complete explanation of reinforcement training available and is used by many professional dog trainers as an aid in solving training problems and developing new training projects.

21 Days to a Trained Dog by Dick Maller and Jeffrey Feinman. Simon and Schuster, 1977. $5.95 in paperback.

There are many good books on dog training. This one, written from the perspective of reinforcement training, is by a leading dog trainer and a psychologist. Contains good tips on training other behavior your Frisbee dog should know, using shaping and reinforcement.

How to Raise a Puppy You Can Live With by Clarice Rutherford and David H. Neil. Alpine Publications, Inc., 1901 S. Garfield, Loveland, CO 80537. $4.95.

A helpful guide to making a dog's first year more bearable for everyone.

Behavior Problems in Dogs by William E. Campbell. American Veterinary Publications, Drawer KK, Santa Barbara, CA 93102. $20.00.

A useful and amusing book covering practically everything dogs can do wrong, why they do it, and how to fix it. Campbell's puppy selection test alone is invaluable (see below).

Frisbee by Judy Horowitz and Billy Bloom. Available from Disc Wares Unlimited, Inc., P. O. Box 333, Amherst, MA 01004. $9.95.

A basic book on learning to play Frisbee, with some information on dogs. Amusingly written; lots of pictures.

Frisbee Players Handbook by Mark Danna and Dan Poynter. Available from Disc Wares Unlimited, Inc., P. O. Box 333, Amherst, MA 01004. $6.95.

Judged by Frisbee experts to be the most comprehensive report on Frisbee play, with extensive instructional material.

Frisbee Sports and Games by Charles Tips and Dan Roddick. Celestial Arts, 231 Adrian Road, Millbrae, CA 94030. $5.95.

All the different things people can do with a Frisbee, including the rules for ten official sports, twenty other disc games, and a wealth of information on throwing skills and strategies. Lots of photos and diagrams.

PAMPHLETS AND OTHER PUBLICATIONS

"Behavior Rx for Selecting a Puppy" by William E. Campbell. Pamphlet available from veterinarians or from Dog Owner Guidance Service, 487 Penny Lane, Grants Pass, OR 97528.

"How to Teach Your Dog to Catch a Frisbee Disc." Pamphlet published by Gaines dog food manufacturers, sponsors of the

Ashley Whippet Invitational tournaments. Available free from Gaines, with a stamped, self-addressed envelope. Send request to Gaines Ashley Whippet Invitational Booklet, P.O. Box 8177, Kanakee, IL 60902.

Dog care and nutritional advice as well as Frisbee-throwing and training tips, and tournament information.

"Frisbee Training for Your Dog" by Daryl Breese. *Dog World,* (January 1984), 300 West Adams St., Chicago, IL 60606. Available from K-9 Disc Masters, Route 4, Box 445C, Bakersfield, CA 93309. $1.00.

Disc Sports: The International Magazine for Flying Disc Sports. Disc Wares Unlimited, Inc., P. O. Box 333, Amherst, MA 01004. Six issues yearly; subscriptions $7.00 a year.

Tournaments, clubs, articles, ads, product evaluations, and so on, all related to Frisbee sports.

K-9 Disc Masters Newsletter edited by Daryl Breese. Route 4, Box 445C, Bakersfield, CA 93309. Free with yearly membership in K-9 Disc Masters; membership fee $10.

Frisbee-dog competition notes, lots of training tips and ideas, low-cost source of practice discs and other training equipment.

Clubs and Organizations

K-9 Disc Masters
Route 4, Box 445C
Bakersfield, CA 93309

Ashley Whippet Invitational
    Headquarters
P. O. Box 1683
Encino, CA 91426
Telephone 1-800-423-3268;
    in California, 818-780-4915

Note: Many clubs, associations, and newsletters exist for Frisbee games played by people, not dogs, such as Ultimate Frisbee and Frisbee Golf, and for collectors of Frisbees. For information on these clubs, contact Frisbee equipment dealers or the following:

Dan Roddick
Director, Sports Promotion
Wham-O, Inc.
835 E. El Monte Street
P. O. Box 4
San Gabriel, CA 91778
Telephone 213-287-9681

Equipment Sources

Discovering the World   Master Card, Visa accepted
Ron Kaufman   Mail, phone, and C.O.D. orders
P. O. Box 125
Davis, CA 95617
Telephone 916-756-DISC

The biggest flying-disc emporium going, with a fat mail-order catalogue full of tips, jokes, and news. Books, T-shirts, mini Frisbees, and over 100 different weights, styles, and sizes of flying discs for different purposes. Of special interest to dog owners: soft Frisbees for safe indoor play, $3.00 each; extra-tough "chomp-resistant" discs, Voit K-9 Vectors, $5.00 each.

Disc Wares Unlimited   Master Card, Visa Accepted
P. O. Box 333
Amherst, MA 01004
Phone 413-253-5674

Discs, tournament equipment, T-shirts, and so forth, all professionally tested. Quantity discounts available. Money-back guarantee. Mail-order catalogue on request or included in *Disc Sports* magazine.

K-9 Disc Masters
Route 4, Box 445C
Bakersfield, CA 93309

This club of Frisbee-dog owners sells practice Frisbees in quantities of 25, 50, or 100, at .59 each, and 4-inch mini Frisbees, ideal for smaller dogs, at .49 each in quantities of 10, 25, or 50. Also available for $9.95 is the "Whip-it" hand-held distance thrower for people who can't throw as far as their dog can run.

About the Author

Karen Pryor pursues two careers: as a scientist and as a writer. Educated at Cornell University, with graduate work in zoology at the University of Hawaii, New York University, and Rutgers, she was a founder of Hawaii's Sea Life Park and Oceanic Institute, where her work with porpoises established her as an authority on learning and training as well as on marine-mammal behavior. She has lectured widely on her research to both lay and scientific audiences, and serves as a consultant to several government agencies and private industry. Her first book, *Nursing Your Baby*, has sold more than 2 million copies. She is a contributor to *New York* magazine, *Psychology Today*, *Omni*, *Reader's Digest*, and other periodicals. The mother of three grown children, Ted, Michael, and Gale Pryor, she is married to Jon Lindbergh and lives in the foothills of the Cascade Mountains in the state of Washington.